KU-379-732

SOMETHING FOR THE GHOSTS

DAVID CONSTANTINE

BLOODAXE BOOKS

Copyright © David Constantine 2002

ISBN: 1 85224 590 5

First published 2002 by
Bloodaxe Books Ltd,
Highgreen,
Tarset,
Northumberland NE48 1RP.

www.bloodaxebooks.com
For further information about Bloodaxe titles
please visit our website or write to
the above address for a catalogue.

Bloodaxe Books Ltd acknowledges
the financial assistance of Northern Arts.

LEGAL NOTICE

All rights reserved. No part of this book may be
reproduced, stored in a retrieval system, or
transmitted in any form, or by any means, electronic,
mechanical, photocopying, recording or otherwise,
without prior written permission from Bloodaxe Books Ltd.

Requests to publish work from this book
must be sent to Bloodaxe Books Ltd.

David Constantine has asserted his right under
Section 77 of the Copyright, Designs and Patents Act 1988
to be identified as the author of this work.

Cover printing by J. Thomson Colour Printers Ltd, Glasgow.

Printed in Great Britain by
Cromwell Press Ltd, Trowbridge, Wiltshire.

SOMETHING FOR THE GHOSTS

David Constantine was born in 1944 in Salford, Lancashire. He read Modern Languages at Wadham College, Oxford, and lectured in German at Durham from 1969 to 1981 and at Oxford from 1981 to 2000. He is a Fellow of the Queen's College, Oxford, and works as a freelance writer and translator.

His first book of poems, *A Brightness to Cast Shadows* (Bloodaxe Books, 1980), was widely acclaimed. His second collection, *Watching for Dolphins* (Bloodaxe Books, 1983), won the 1984 Alice Hunt Bartlett Prize, and his academic study, *Early Greek Travellers and the Hellenic Ideal* (Cambridge University Press, 1984), won the first Runciman Prize in 1985. His first novel, *Davies*, was published by Bloodaxe in 1985, and his first book of stories, *Back at the Spike* by Ryburn Publishing in 1994. *Fields of Fire*, his biography of Sir William Hamilton, was published by Weidenfeld & Nicolson in 2001.

His third collection, *Madder* (Bloodaxe Books, 1987), a Poetry Book Society Recommendation, won the Southern Arts Literature Prize. The French edition of *Madder*, translated by Yves Bichet as *Sorlingues* (Éditions La Dogana, 1992), won the Prix Rhône-Alpes du Livre. His *Selected Poems* (Bloodaxe Books, 1991) is a Poetry Book Society Recommendation. His latest collections are: *Caspar Hauser: a poem in nine cantos* (Bloodaxe Books, 1994); *The Pelt of Wasps* (Bloodaxe Books, 1998), which includes his verse-play *Lady Hamilton and the Elephant Man*, first broadcast on BBC Radio 3 in 1997; and *Something for the Ghosts* (Bloodaxe Books, 2002).

He has published translations of poetry and prose by German, French and Greek writers. His critical introduction to the poetry of Friedrich Hölderlin appeared from Oxford University Press in 1988, and his translation of Hölderlin's *Selected Poems* from Bloodaxe Books in 1990, winning the European Poetry Translation Prize for its revised edition (1996). He has also translated Goethe's novel *Elective Affinities* (Oxford University Press, World's Classics, 1994) and Kleist's *Selected Writings* (Dent, 1997). The Bloodaxe Contemporary French Poets series includes his translations of (with Helen Constantine) *Spaced, Displaced* by Henri Michaux (1992) and (with Mark Treharne) *Under Clouded Skies / Beauregard* by Philippe Jaccottet (1994). His translation of Hans Magnus Enzensberger's latest collection *Lighter Than Air* is forthcoming from Bloodaxe, and his new version of Goethe's *Faust* from Penguin Classics.

'To our bodies turn we then...'

Acknowledgements

Acknowledgements are due to the editors of the following publications in which some of these poems first appeared: *Atlanta Review, Gravesiana, The Interpreter's House, Metre, Orbis, Oxford Poetry, Oxford Magazine, The North, PN Review, Poetry London, Poetry Review, The Reader* and *The Shop*. 'School Parties in the Museum' was commissioned by the Salisbury Festival 1999 and published in their anthology *Last Words* (Picador, 1999). 'The Immortals of Landevennec' was commissioned and broadcast by BBC Radio 3 for the Proms 2000.

Contents

Nude

How simple it is: day knocks
And somebody opens, the shutter opens in
And in come light and warmth together as one and the same
And where she stands
Is neither a circle of privacy
Nor the arena of a performance
But only a small round mat for her feet on the cold tiles
While under an empty mirror
She bows to the water lifted in her hands
And sideways on her sunlight comes in from the garden
And on her back there is a man's admiration.

You will say it is only a picture, another nude
But I say it has been that simple:
Jug, basin, washstand, towel and chair
The plain nouns, and a woman at a meeting place
Of warm sunlight and loving admiration
And easy feeling both.

Something for the Ghosts

Here's something for the ghosts who are
No one now and can't come up against
The edge of anyone else: that heavy skirt,
Your bare cold feet come out from under it,
Their print, black wet, on the slabs of slate

For days. Poor ghosts, where they are mine and thine
Flit like snowflakes, drift like mist, not like
My grasp of your black hair, the rain in it,
The smell of the rain that I breathed in after
For days. Poor gibbering ghosts, when they have done

Their best with bits of sound to shape someone
They knew or thought they knew or wished they had
It never amounts to anything more than this
Ghost of a mouth with questions in such as
Who were you and who did you think I was?

Dear Reader

His first morning, theirs together the first,
A white mist filled the deep hospital garden
Even to the lip of her windows
All the arrangement gone in a silent boiling

On and on went the mist into the open country
All the particularities went under it
As far as the hills that she had promised me
And they were all alone like a school of islands

As far away as moons. In that condition
She sank again into the trance of reading
His head had interrupted
One long novel adding upon another

Like a child in winter, perhaps convalescent,
And the shadows of people who loved her came and went
And while he fed and slept and fed
Her eyes were on a page, her fingers left

The soft pulse of his silky fontanelle
To turn another page. She agreed with him
That he must thrive and smiled and winced at his savage focusing
On her and loved him best

When he slipped from her nipple back into the welter
Of nothing belonging yet, no shape, no form,
And she began again in another situation
Somewhere not here, in at the seeding,

Sexing, naming, in at the jostling
Of destinies against their author, she was merciless
On females wistful over roads not taken
And coming to an ending she undid the knot

And slept among the fray of possibilities
The white mist feeling for a slit of warmth
The level solvent going on and on
As far as the hills that lay apart, shining.

The House

You won't forget the house
Will you? I never will.
The south wind rattled the sash
And rain came in on the sill

And the wind denuded the moon
White and the white of the tide
Wheeling into the wind
Lifted, showed and frayed

And the sun came out of the sea
And all that way across
Easily found the house,
The bed, the looking-glass.

Remember the house so well
That somebody else elsewhere
Will say, 'We had a house
The same as where you were

But a hundred miles from the sea
And it was the north that blew
And the sky was as sheer as steel
And everything flared and flew

Stubble went down the wind
The oaks were filled with a voice
And the stars in the Milky Way
Screamed like a slide of ice

And the sun that found our bed
Rose over oaks and a hill
But the house was surely the same
Except for the sash and the sill

And there was a looking-glass
And though they were mine and hers
The faces shown by the sun
Might have been hers and yours

You remember it all so well
That except for the south and the sea
That was surely the house
Except for her and me.'

Sleepwalker

I watched her window from a vantage point.
The sash was pushed up, with the daylight,
Very early, came a steady breeze.
The gap, the blowing through, and her white curtains:
Easy to imagine that she ran towards me
Or that she had flitted for ever
And day and night changing and any weather
Could visit as they liked now and would make no difference.
But I did my level best to think of her asleep
With an open face and open palms
Fast asleep in the summer early daylight
The outdoors streaming coolly over body and soul
Asleep under the inrush of good spirits
Whose shape for entering was the light curtains
Their being raised and flounced and almost steadily laid out
Slant to their quivering limits at her bed. Easy to imagine
Tide-set my way and all
The lovely underwater waking dress and hair
Streaming back. I watched and watched
And I suppose that I was trusting some deep warning
Such as swifts have in their sleeping downward spirals
That I would quit and be gone back into hiding
Before any strangers came.

Man and Wife

He wakes like someone shouted for, she lies
After in the violent lights thinking am I
Invisible, am I already dead?
Trying not to let her ghost go after his
Into the wind and the rain or under the sharp stars
With coughing foxes. He has phoned the police
To say if ever they catch him in their beams
Lopsided, savage and helpless as a badger
To let him be, it's not against the law
To walk the old road between the sea and the marsh
And listen at gaps and holes in the sand dunes
For what it really sounds like, and to get in
As far as he can without sinking, in among
Countless thousand starlings fastened on the reeds
And listen, if that is trespassing, so what?
Who cares? She does, she thinks they should lock him up
For his own good, for hers, for everyone's:
Eavesdropper, voyeur, night after night
Trying to see things as though he were dead and gone,
Trying to be slantways on, trying to get behind,
To be in the deep unease of the marsh and not
Interfere and witness the sea as it used to be
When nothing was watching but the stars. He comes home
A secret way over the old mines, over terrain
Probed and tunnelled and thoroughly gone into
And now for ever liable to sudden appearances
Of wells of water in which the yellow moon
Or a fearful human peers. She draws the curtains
And sees him mounted like a scarecrow on the boundary hedge.
She cannot make him a sign of recognition.
Perhaps he has found how far under their dwelling
The old galleries go, he is watching the tabs
On things, the sounds for house and home, come off
And blow away, he wishes it, traitor, accomplice
He has got beyond the pale and night after night now
Against house and home he will side with the wind.

On the Cliffs, Boscastle

The bulk, thin flora, hunched here like a crow,
Sky red as poppy, black
As the heart of a poppy, some long way below
Slop slop, the constant cuffing of the sea.

Not sensible, too perilous, watching black
Burst slowly from the heart. If fell,
More like a brainless stone, not like a crow.
The red sops up the black. It welcomes it.

Fiddle in a cavity top left with a stalk of last year's thrift,
Meanwhile a black detachment troops away,
Sniff at the stick, gawp at the ghosts, sniff, sniff,
Already its little virtue has gone off it.

Get back, on hands and knees snuffling a track
While there's still blood in the sky, get back
To the B & B and your scented mate
Between silk sheets after her bath, get her on you

To practise, practise, practise the kiss of life.

Monologue
or
The Five Lost Géricaults

*(In the last years of his life Géricault did ten portraits
of monomaniacs. Only five have survived. My four
characters, and their narrator, might be those lost.)*

Commander Olleranshaw at Number 33,
With him it's dogshit, he's out every day
Chalking a ring round every load he finds
And sticking a flag in it, such lovely hands
He has, like a brain surgeon's, poor man
While everyone sensible's watching television
He's in behind his curtains making little flags
And muttering how many tons of dogshit dogs
Do every day. Don't get me wrong: he's right,
I've counted fifty flags just on our street
Between here and the Post Office: times that
By all the streets in Eccles and you'll get
Some idea of the problem and of course
That's only Eccles. No, what I meant was
I'd hate to wake with only one thing on the brain
Every morning, it must be terrible, I mean
There's more to life than your one big idea
However big. That woman's another,
'Sins of the World' I call her, still in bed
Her duty opens like an 'A to Z',
The bits all finish in another bit
And if she ever got to the end of it,
Which she won't, she'd have to start again,
Us being the way we are, she's grown
A special nail for lifting wrappers with
Or bus tickets, for getting underneath
One of their edges when the wet has stuck them flat,
I watched her half an hour clawing like that
On one of my off days, walking, walking, follow
That madman Olleranshaw you hear him bellow
And curse the world to hell but follow her
Just soft tut-tuts, she's like a creature
Only come about because the duty did,

And went by evolution the shape needed –
Humped, with a shoulder up, and swagged with bags,
Tut-tut, pick-pick, scrape-scrape, it plagues
My nights thinking how many bags you'd fill
If you took it seriously after the Council
Has given up, I think of terrible places,
The bus stop where they chuck their takeaways
And outside school and how the winter
Under the hedges shows how bad we are
And think of the graveyard rolling with empties,
Prickly with needles, slippy with condoms – suppose,
I think, she ever thinks of that, dear God
Better by far she got it into her head
Her duty ran to shovelling up the things
With flags in in that madman's rings
Only not what's littering our cemetery.
Now wouldn't you think that any God of Mercy
Worth His salt would send her deepest snow
One early morning, snow on snow on snow,
So she'd see cleanliness on earth for once
Or Jesus give her something for her conscience
In the wine, a worming thing, in the loving cup
Some efficacious dose to make it stop
Whispering through the miles of her insides
She'll never do well enough however hard she tries?
Poor Sins of the World, the world or her
One of us will have to change and it won't be her,
Barring miracles. These people,
They ask a lot of us. For example
That chap who's always smiling at everyone,
His trouble is he wants nothing bad to happen,
Smiling, nodding, bowing at anyone
The bad might come from, which is everyone,
And making little magic jerks, his trouble is
He wants no one to notice him, he says:
'I'm nobody, I'm nothing, I'm not here
To speak of hardly, please don't bother
Your boot with me, don't trouble your fist',
He wants to be like them in with the rest
Where the bad might come from not outside
Where it's coming to. Bright-eyed
Mr Smiley with the very eager face

Some days he has to turn away and practise.
I suppose those are his very fearful days.
I hear him saying 'after you' and 'please,
No, after you' and 'thank you, thank you, thank you'
And 'sorry', the way we do, only more so,
All that rehearsing to sound ordinary
So when he speaks the world won't say 'Who's he?
Who's this queer chap, why don't we tar
And feather him, poor chap, why don't we saw
His head off slowly and stick it on a pole
And why's he wet?' I nod, I bow, I smile,
I roll my hands at him, 'Cheer up,' I say,
'Nothing bad might happen and almost certainly
Not as bad as that and saying please all day
Won't help and practising and anyway
You do it very well.' Funny round here,
When you weigh up, how many folk go queer.
There's that lad living at the yellow door
Though lad's not right, nor living, it's more
Like falling what he does, the way things do
In outer space, comets or angels, falling slow
But falling, surely falling. Anyway
With him it's bicycles. I counted twenty-three
Downstairs, all wrecks except for two,
One ladies' and one kiddies', they're brand new
And bought, he says, the rest he nicked or found,
Frames on the stairs and handlebars around
The toilet and his bed, bikes without wheels
Like little crippled horses. I say it's bicycles
But the other thing he does is fall in love
With girls who'll speak to him and several have
Over the years within a radius
Of fifty miles of his double bed and his
Graveyard of bikes, most recently
In Diggle one in the Public Library,
He rode to see her on a Raleigh Twelve Speed,
One working, high, no brakes, and waited.
Nobody waits like him, I've watched him wait
Hours outside a teashop in Gallowgate
Where another works who spoke to him.
'The trouble is,' I said, 'you frighten them.'
'All I want's some female talking with,' he said.

I thought of the little radio by his bed,
In it more like, and his finger fiddling at
The tiny tuning wheel in hopes he'll get
Some female still awake at 3 a.m.
Who'll speak. Trouble is he frightens them –
Straight limbs, clear skin, long curls – honest to God
The word for him I should have used's not lad
But youth, lost youth, angel
Falling, falling. That's what the women smell:
Pheromones of loneliness, a musk of fear
Of falling further, further, further, further,
That's how he waits outside the library,
Outside the teashop and that's what they see,
The women he loves: the abyss. He'll pull me in
With eyes like that if I speak to him again.
The hands give you away, so do the shoes
But most of all it's in the eyes it shows
What's eating you, some days it seems to me
Half's staring at the other half, very hungry
Even in the café or especially there,
Or perhaps it's only Eccles. That writer,
I call him that though I've never seen him write,
The way he looks and hugs his scribbles tight
In a bundle two feet thick, he's like a bear
The way he growls in his overcoat and hair
And beard that have got so long they've given up.
It makes me itch to look at him, can't stop
Looking across at him, whatever the heat
That hair, that overcoat, however sweet
And light yourself might be he makes you sweat
Only looking at him. Last week, the worst I've had
Lately, I took my tea across, I said:
'For Christ's sake take your coat off, sit and write
Something, here's a pen, here's a clean white sheet,
Sit still, stop scratching, write something,
All you do in here is sit there mumbling
And hugging that.' 'No fucking good,' he said,
'Can't do it, can't speak a word that's good
Next to another word, can't even say,
So that it makes you cry out loud, the way
That girl serving watches the clock and the door
About now when that lad will come in or

He won't, I mean the dread she's in he won't
Or will, her exact way of suffering, I can't
Say even that so that it hurts, that's how
No fucking good I am.' 'Then why, I'd like to know,
Do your hug your bundle like a honeypot?'
'Because,' he said, 'it's all I've fucking got,
It's what I've done, it's what I can't still do,
Not even that, and that was no good too.'
'I see,' I said. 'So you sit and itch instead?'
'Sweat, scratch and itch,' he said, 'until I'm dead.'

Dramatis Personae

1 *Chorus*

Not much of a role, on the sidelines
Moaning over Somebody Else's error
And always worried something worse would happen
Which it always did. Mostly we got things wrong:
Asked the gods (the wrong gods) for a particular mercy
That was the worst imaginable affliction
As it turned out. How they must have laughed.
We were continually amazed. 'Well, I never did!'
And 'Fancy that!' were our catchphrases.
We had less gumption than the Servant
And far less understanding than the Messenger
And never (thank God) saw into the heart of life
The way Somebody Else did. We talked a lot
But it never prevented anything
Or comforted those going to the slaughter
And our summings-up were so laborious
And events in such a hurry
Often, to be honest, we lost the plot.
But we gave the language some memorable sayings:
'Cheer up, it might never happen', for example,
And 'When in doubt, do nowt'.

2 *Servant*

What happened any fool could see it would.
Do this, it will. They did, and so it did
And in they went up to their necks wide-open-eyed
When any blind man could have told them don't.
Always in public too, they had no shame,
Our lords, they thumped their children, laid about
Their wives, swore terrible oaths what they
Would do to every mortal soul if this
Or that, so help them God, amen, which is
Asking for it. Always in front of us
Who stood there like the furniture until

One of our betters said fetch him, kill her,
Clean up. Did no one ever teach them, On
Your own head be it, what you reap you sow,
Don't piss into the wind? Or any manners?
We stood there watching for the Messenger.
Then how they roared, always in public too,
And flailed around and tore their hair and stabbed
Their eyes and cut their bollocks off and said
Some god has done this, friends, oh see, some god
Has made me mad. Some god, my arse.

3 *Messenger*

Spare a thought for me. I brought the news
Which was always bad and all the worse in the end
If it ever looked good. From somewhere offstage
Me and my news as fast as possible
Were always getting nearer. Meanwhile onstage
The lords were continuing as though it had not happened
But it already had, the star was dead,
I was the last light, travelling, travelling,
And in the space before the scream began
I got my message into shape, so with decorum
To spill the guts. I was the word that kills
In person. Sometimes on my announcement
Came the sight itself: a lord with the staggers,
Blood in the lovely apples of the eyes,
Dead progeny. Spare a thought for me,
I was there, I was everywhere
Where the worst came true, I saw the lot,
It was my job to bring it home to you,
I have it all by heart still, every line.

Mosaics in the Imperial Palace

Maximianus with eyes of marble oversees
The transportation of the animals out of Africa
Across a sea awash with divinities
And stuff to eat. He stands on the littoral

At an entrance wound into Africa
And the beasts are like a bleeding that will never stop
So long as the vast heart pumps
And it will for ever. In the old world by now

There is less shade for travellers on the highways
And for the beasts less hiding, but Africa
Is an eternal covert and the sea
No human engine will ever sieve it out.

Maximianus has seen everything or enough
To pre-empt the rest. *Nil admirari.*
It is all one: John Dories and the pearly unicorn,
Jackals and spouting tritons. Pitiless

To the Big Top animals trussed, spiked,
And hauled up gangplanks by their tender snouts
And to the monsters pitiless
Who are so encumbered by their heads and horns

And so bewildered by the common daylight
That man the hunter easily presses them
For Rome. Maximianus is not amused
Even by Orpheus and his myriad games

Of mixing: human babes
With wings riding the dolphins; a centaur
Trotting with a gift; a griffin smiling. Orpheus
Playing Cupid between the kinds: a lady

In her mirror showing a white rhinoceros
Their good looks. Watery Orpheus
Practising sympathy and dissolution, shapes
Unshaping, the restless slop and throw

Of drafts and chances, trials of fins and feelers,
The cleft thighs closing in a mermaid,
Leviathan turning with a wink
Into a tippling horn of plenty.

Maximianus Herculius supposes
That Rome's belly and Rome's eyes
Will gorge for ever on the sea and on Africa
And if not there are other Africas

To bleed as many beasts and wonders
As there are sprats in other seas
Or tesserae in the marble mountains
For man the maker to record that it was so.

Dominion

Dear God, if you can imagine us, Man,
Without a chain-saw in our hands or the gun
Or looking away from the prices on the screen
For half a minute, even then in that
Even by you perhaps unimaginable state

The truth is we're not good enough, never were,
Never will be, we're not fit, we don't fit in,
Nothing will live with us except the viruses
And dogs and lice, nothing likes us down here,
Everything else is subtler, finer, fitter than us.

Take a coral reef: we come visiting
It gives up the ghost, it's a boneyard by morning,
Spectral groves. And that's us all over,
The ashes, the fallout, whatever we come near
Even in white, with a gauze over the gob,

We're the kiss of death. Dear God, that day
In Eden when you made Adam boss
What a catastrophe, even you must see it by now,
Anything would have been better than us,
A dodo, for example, a booby, a diplodocus.

The Llandudno Town Band

High water behind them the town band
Give us a tune while the sun goes down
Which it does too soon
Leaving us cold in the lee of the big headland

The old and the very old in stripy deckchairs
Recumbent under wraps like a year ago
And some drawn up alongside in flash new wheelchairs
The same old crowd, minus the passed away,

Huddling together on the big prom
Under the vast sky here we are again:
Sacred on Sundays and the profane
Mondays, Wednesdays and Fridays, always at 8 p.m.

Against the surf, under the cackling gulls
What a brave noise they make, it cheers me up no end:
Fatty the Tuba with the very thick spectacles
Ballooning fast, and his lady friend

(I call her his lady friend) blowing him kisses
The length of her brassy trombone
And two very pretty things, sex unknown,
Winking over their cornets in white blouses.

The gulls jeer and a shrewd wind blows
And but for the plastic clothes pegs in nine bright colours
Away would go the tunes from the shows
Like all the other litter of our yesteryears.

To finish, Dave the conductor promises a solo
But doesn't say it's Sally on the flugelhorn
Or Bob on sax and the regulars know
It's him himself and he'll suddenly turn

And it won't be the twiddling stick he'll hold
But the trumpet and there he'll swell
Facing us all, full frontal
And such a sound will come forth, pure gold

Out of his silver, and not the Last Post
Nor the Last Trump either though I grant you an angel
Recording on the Orme would think it must
Be Jehoshaphat down here – no, our Dave'll

Close his eyes and deliver what he can hear
In his head or his heart or up there in the sky
And give it us neat, give it us proof and pure
On and on, in and in, till every body

And in every body the huddled soul
Shy as an embryo
Hearkens. Then that's it for now,
That's it till Sunday and *Abide With Me* and all

Not stiff for ever get to their feet
And the wheelchair-riders sit up straight
And the team in purple sound and tinkle the tune
For us to hum *Land of My Fathers* and sing *God Save the Queen*

And we do our best but it's not much cop
Against the whole of the Irish Sea
Come very close. The band pack up,
It's cold, the wheelchairs speed away.

Encouragements

One devoted lunatic, I forget who,
Said if he closed his eyes on the right night,
Cloudless of course, every five years or so
And lifted his bare face and kept his eyes shut tight

And said how lucky he was and how grateful
He felt a touch of warmth from her face on his face
Down a quarter of a million miles of empty space
And on these rare surrenders he got by pretty well.

But another, again I forget who,
Said to hell with charity, he lived in hopes of cruelty:
The sudden conviction of a door opening behind you,
Ice down the spine, you turn to look, and she

Is leaning under the lintel with nothing on.
The smile. The 'How about this?' And gone.

Drunk Locked in Music Room Wrecks Grand

The five holes of his sometime face had run.
His voice came up like an experiment,
Gas over phlegm. He wanted out, it said.
A night like this? Moon like a burning glass
Of cold, snow hard as quartz, the wet
Between his legs would set fast like cement.

But still he wanted out. He must have heard.
Why else not lie low in our cubbyhole
Sleeping and thieving biscuits till a door opened?
He had overheard. One lug cocked like a fox's
Had let the spirits in to wriggle through
The labyrinth for his white bit of soul.

He must have woken to the aftermath
The pause after a blessing while it lasts
The silence filling up with pearly light
And under the Masters with their scrolls and quills
Still listening he dragged the body in
And then his howl began. He could still hear

Order in something fleet and sylph as streams,
Reprises, a looping up again, a sweet
Forgiving try again insistence,
A laving clean, a coming back for stragglers,
A lifting up, a carrying to an end
And then beyond an end, I overheard

The howl, the roar, the man tearing apart
Because he felt his bit of soul panic
Like a lad in a flue, that night so cold and still
Across the city you could hear the farthest bell
And sleep, knowing what o'clock, knowing all is well,
And then he ceased and then the worse began,

The appassionato smashing, such a while
It seems to me still hearing it the teeth endured
And chattered, all the breaking teeth and all
The inner booming over his Weep! Weep!
I came in like the jailor with my keys.
Our brass was in his hand. He wanted out.

Catacombs, Paris

Collecting the photos at the counter next to where
She bought the testing kit he sees what he has done,
She has, they have, down there
In the deepest circle by the font that one
Script called the Samaritan Woman's Well
And the other Lethe. She is displayed
Much like a nude against the knobby wall
Of end-on femurs and humeri, arms wide
Along a dado curve of skulls. Boudoir
Or chapel apse in a kraal of bone of some
Few hundred of several millions of dead,
His lens, the flash, her look of centre spread.
The place? Down there. And when? The morning after
One of his several million sperm went home.

Town Centre

Some drunks upset me, it's the way they sit
Placidly vacant in the public place
Or one who puts his hands together in a prayer
And lays his head on it, where does he think he is
With his cherub snout? That boy under the clock

Upsets me too, turning, turning, he is so on show
With his heart on his sleeve and love writ
Large and hopeless over his silly face
Now she won't come. Here where the milling is
And we dance and stamp we don't want stumbling blocks

We don't want drunks and lovers under our feet
And now that widow outside the United Friendly
Puzzling over an absence in her open shopping bag
She makes another hole in the heart of the place
That wants filling in, and what with?

Mel

Mel wants to be an actress.
And be looked at, Mel?
But it wouldn't be me they would be looking at.

Or a beautician:
Ladies' faces under her gentle hands
Making ladies happier with the way they look.

Mel has razored her lashes off.
From wrist to shoulder bone
She has ruled in all the degrees with a razor blade.

Mel with her stripes
Mel with her bald eyes
Her nightmare is a precinct of Saturday people

Suddenly turning from their fun and their purposes
To look at Mel. She has a pet rabbit
And a guardian angel.

Their looks are kind.
Nothing between a rabbit and an angel
Looks kindly enough on Mel.

She has done me a picture in her English book
Of what it feels like being Mel.
She appears as a naked dolorosa

Fuller of daggers than the mother was.
She looks at me
I fear she will show herself in the shopping mall like that

One Saturday afternoon, with lidless eyes.

J

J has been studying the tyranny
The lengths they went:
A tapeworm, for example.

She composes a letter to *Vogue* on behalf of her speechless sisters
Sign this, she commands.

J knows.

J in the mirror without her clothes
Eggshell, x-ray.
She has parted company with the moon
But sideways on
How far she is still from the line of the clean needle
Its minimal eye
How grossly far.

She would teach her belly obedience
But her belly is a ward of court.

She composes a letter to Doctor Fatman
The force-feeder
Who thinks he knows.

Legger

Casting him off from the sympathetic horses
They shoved him gently into the low hole
Telling him the drift, such as it was, would help him
And that the level of the water would not rise or fall.

He went in snug as a shuttle with a lantern in the bows
About as bright as the light on a glow-worm's tail
And lay on his back the way they had said he must
And began to leg his longboat through the hill

Mile after mile, only as fast as Shanks's
And the sun came and went and the same old stars
Shifted their quarters slowly as it is fixed they will
And he continued his course out of sight of theirs

Treading the slimy ceiling in his hobnail boots
Like a living dead as though to slide the lid
He trod and trod and the heavy water
Squeezed past him with a shudder on either side.

I have had a picnic on that sunny hill
And read 'The Lady of Shalott' to a romantic girl
Hoping it would undress her and lay her down
Smiling under my shadow and my smile

And all the while those thousands of fathoms down
Under the severed ends of sinister lodes
His legs even in his dreams, even dead asleep,
Were trudging along the roof of his one and only road

Long since without even a fag end of light
Even the kindness of dumb animals long since gone from mind
Under the weight of millions of years of rock
And twenty hundred of christian humankind.

He will be a wonder when he comes out of the hill
On our side berthing in the orange water
In the old wharfs among the sunken skeletons
Of the ancient narrowboats, strange as Arthur

In his overalls and the soles of his boots and the soles
Of his feet worn through and no light in his eyes
Under the interest of our savants and our developers
Grinning with horror, rictus of the bad old days.

The Immortals of Landevennec

Ripe with years and over-ripe
    The latest breath they took
However thin was never the last
    And when they slept, they woke.

They were under a hole in heaven's floor
    And from it by day and by night
The light of everlasting life
    Fell on them like a blight.

Through the Judas-trap in heaven's floor
    They could see the radiant dead
Like mirrors mounting up and up
    To a light that might be God.

But where they were, on their terrain,
    They could not live or die.
No heart, no muscle, and their poor souls
    Sick for the hole in the sky.

Inching after death they stayed
    Beneath the dead above
Until in pity or disgust
    An angel told them: Move.

Miraculous, the rush of strength
    To unbuild and build again
Their walls and roof and plant their plots
    Out of sight of heaven

A stone's throw west, nearer the sea,
    Under a normal sky
Where they rejoined the way of life
    And they began to die

In turn, always the oldest first,
    You might say courteously,
As though a fitting thing at last
    Was here allowed to be.

For here the earth was debonair
    And blessed and full of grace.
She turned a little stream their way
    To aid the growing place.

Below their walls, above the sea,
    She brought to light a well.
The sweet was bedded on the salt
    And with it rose and fell.

The stag stood at the chapel door,
    The swallows entered in,
All the needy creatures came
    As though to kith and kin.

The sad immortals housing now
    Out of heaven's way
And free to leave, the sweet earth gave
    Them grounds on which to stay.

Like breath on frost they saw her scent
    Above the wetted thorn
In sun the shivering of her heat
    Above the blonde corn

And through their shining majuscules
    The Green Man shoved his head
And down their margins sprouted lines
    On lovers wanting bed.

The Senator

Sleepless, he asks for the car and an exeat
And slides by moonlight to the usual place
Behind the Palace, the Peace Allée,
Statues among the orange trees, halts at the space

He chose for his. From cap to boot he is as white
As orange blossom or a first communion
Except where he has blackened around the eyes
Like the Palace marble when the shells went in.

Sees her: blacker than a bad tooth in the gap
For his white replica, a mother or one
In love who never did become a mother,
Girl as was, one age now with the eternal crone.

He lifts a white glove against the usual photograph
('These sons and lovers lifted up at me
Like permits to beg, who posed them all,
That trash, so they look like Jesus?') But she

'Senator,' she says, 'may you live long,
A long long eventide in the bosom of the nation.'
What does she know? What has she guessed of his days?
Words of a blessing in the voice of malediction.

Daily, after mass, punctilious young men,
Steely young women, the researchers come,
Younger than his many grandchildren,
They want help with the new curriculum

Or they bring maps, the latest printing,
Spotted with icons for a camp, a cellar,
A pit, and, by magnitude, stars for the clusters.
'Senator,' they ask, 'is that where?'

And lists, always the lists, and photographs,
Often they are photographs of before and after.
They hand him a magnifying glass. 'Look closely.
That face, was that a usual procedure?'

The medals he issued return at every post
Mostly anonymously, but he can tell
From his lists and numbers. 'You too?'
A note sometimes: 'Forgive me. It had begun to smell.'

Every day there are hearings, they are polite,
And excursions in the black car
Or mottled helicopter. So beautiful his land
Looked down upon. 'Is that where they are?'

'Live long,' she says, 'with all of an old man's
Usual ailments, and come here often and see
By moonlight in the soft season how sweet
The city is now, if not for you or me

For the young, for your children's children
Fleeing your name by deed poll, live long
In smells of camp, cellar, pit and daily
The dogshit medals coming home, live on

And stand here often when I have vacated it
In the space you chose, all white except your eyes,
Which will be dark and vast and wormy as your many graves,
Senator, live for ever,' the girl-crone says.

The Grief Coming Out

I heard this from the mother of my dead friend:

How she was sitting still among her ornaments
In a vague discomfort among her photographs
In a vague distress so that she couldn't have said
Where about body and soul it troubled her

When suddenly where there had been a little itching
But nowhere very particular from her wrists and arms
But not from any cut or opening, just so
Blood started out, much blood, and how the doctor
Had said this might be from seven years ago

The grief coming out. There are no witnesses
But I believe her, she sounded so incredulous
As though she had travelled to a primitive shrine
And seen among the silvery ex-votos

This strange effusion happen to a statue.

The Porthleven Man

That Porthleven man keeps coming back to me
Who stood a last round, the usual,
And drank his own up slowly as he always did
And said goodnight one and all and from one and all
Got goodnights back, heartfelt as usual,

But in the cold air turned right not left and slowly,
As he was bound to, went the length of the breakwater
As far as you can go, and further,
And never came up, never came back and his zimmer
Stood there lightly on the edge. Remember

Porthleven, that night, that moon
When the sea came in with most of the horizon
Most of the western hemisphere came in on us
To that one point which is as far as you can go
And planed down the length of the granite breakwater

Like all her dolphins, like one continuous
Making of dolphins and how they rolled and showed
Their bellies to the sleeping port and in
Back into the matrix then, into her sea
Under her pulsing moon gave back,

Always to come again, the dream of them
And very idea? There, then:
Edge, salt, hilarity. All Souls
When his loved ones had given him up for lost
They gathered at opening time on the far end and tossed

Four score and two fiery chrysanths on the black
And level sea. These nights when I wake
The Porthleven man keeps coming back to me.
I need icons, I need people to live up to
Because of your horizons, because of your western sea.

Room Facing Cythera

Because she has a horror of lifts I ascended alone
In that twin coffin of one with the bags to a corridor
Lightless, airless, still as a mortuary
Where I was lost and could not tell which numbers
Which side had the sunless yard and which the sea

Only hope, again, for more than the measure
For more than my deserts again and again
And found her there already turning the key
On a room, an afternoon
More shut to light than the corridor, but she

Like the blinded fending something off
Felt to the window, pushed the wooden lids
And light came in, a bay of it,
All the silver sea of light to Cythera and back
Came in on a southerly, a light

To unclothe in and be shown and seen
From under the arc of the sky unceasingly
Landed in waves. What we did, she and I,
In so much indoor daylight
All down the leisurely slope of that long afternoon

I shut, like crystal in an egg of stone,
In the innermost stanza of my heart. But still
At large, and anyone can hear it, is
The measure of those waves in that place shipping in the light
Neither at bloodpace nor with the long arrival

Of rollers down the Atlantic but in a steady haste
And while I slept all night like one of the blessed
That beat insisted against the slowing of my blood
And still in the morning at the window
When I looked out and found her island gone

In a mist, invisible, unimaginable
The waves, that thudding, though the southerly had ceased
Beat like oars in a quick tempo
And against my heart when I descended, again alone,
Like oars they struck in time towards a certain landfall.

Shabbesgoy

Daylight still, a green sky. At lighting-up time
There was already the thin beginning of a moon, and one star
So that from the streets that smelled of the gasworks and coalfires
And gasps of fighting beer and because of the abattoir
Almost rural he went with clenched fists, wishing hard

Over the river that only transfusions from the factories
Kept going. Or it was winter, fog
In which he left her safe by the street lamp nearest home
Shaped and illumined and vanished immediately
Towards the hospital, its thousand smeared windows.

Him, you. You do not remember, but I say
That on the hill at the big houses waiting for a lamplighter
Or a firemender they never had anyone luckier than you
The boy courting, radiant, burning, for that small service
Out of his trance of vows and wishes accosted courteously

At the gate, passer-by, who lifted his head that wore
The new moon and her star or shone from the drizzled fog
With the aura of apparition. How queer the rules are
High on the slopes above the dead river,
How quick and simple were your offered hands.

The Hoist

The hoist was strange. Going up, the Nurse said,
First floor haberdashery. Stranger than that
Old word haberdashery, the way he dangled
Under the beak of it like a babe arriving,
Mute in a grim patience, his empty mouth
And his eyes tight shut as if he guarded
A fitter idea of himself in a sort of privacy.

A thing to look away from but we gawped
Like clownish witnesses of an ascension
And I thought of an old mad king still gripping
Tatters of divinity around his shoulders
Or one in a tumbril and the old folk crossing themselves
Or a pharaoh, or a lost god, when the Nurse said
Going down, and settled him in the chair and wheeled him off.

Aphasia

He never said much. Less and less in there.
Till nothing. 'But he squoze my hand,' she said,
'And at least he smiled.' His smile! There used to be
A word for it in the childhood of the tongue,
The word 'seely' that came up from the roots
And died but left a ghostly twin, a word
That shifts among the grown-ups still, the word 'silly'.

The stuck for words, I've watched them hit the place
The word should be and find it gone and claw
The air for it and pluck the sheet and close
Their eyes and groan, knowing it's nowhere near
The tip of the tongue but on a piece of once
And no longer terra firma come adrift
Somewhere arctic going mushy in a fog.

Not him. Not then. Come home from being in
Without a word he viewed the garden like
Someone let off, someone let in to where
The things divest. Seely the face
That looks like that, seely the smile on her
Whose talk was lovely rapid like a nymph's become a stream's,
Seely the two in silence like before they knew their names.

Common and Particular

I like these men and women who have to do with death,
Formal, gentle people whose job it is,
They mind their looks, they use words carefully.

I liked that woman in the sunny room
One after the other receiving such as me
Every working day. She asks the things she must

And thanks me for the answers. Then I don't mind
Entering your particulars in little boxes,
I like the feeling she has seen it all before,

There is a form, there is a way. But also
That no one come to speak up for a shade
Is like the last, I see she knows that too.

I'm glad there is a form to put your details in,
Your dates, the cause. Glad as I am of men
Who'll make a trestle of their strong embrace

And in a slot between two other slots
Do what they have to every working day:
Carry another weight for someone else.

It is common. You are particular.

The Anemones

Back here the anemones had died in my big room
Up against the window gaping for daylight
In the long jar scrabbling for drink like children's straws
Like moths the colours of Hades, the crimson, the blue, the black
In rigor mortis sooting the sterile glass
Wide open and raging for water and more light
That is how I found the anemones when I came back.

The Crem

This is a ragged place. Nothing fits.
I suppose the cemetery was put there first
Then someone in Planning, because of the railway
And knowing of the coming of the expressway,
Made it the zone for light industry

With a plot for the crem. The cars arrive
Sighing down the old roads at a decent pace
And leave on the new, unburdened, fast.
Announcements of smoke. This is no place
To come and sit with your trouble in working hours.

The roses mean well but the ashes look ghastly
And the dedicated benches put you on show
On a little hillside, they make you spectators
Of every delivery. But come out of hours
With nobody else to look at it's even worse.

Everything's been tried here and did no good.
There are walls of tablets of stone you can stand and read,
And urns and uprights as though if they could
They'd be next door in the old style, as though
Ash isn't enough. Lately there's cellophane

And dead bouquets on the earth like murdered birds.
They look a mess but the Council lets them lie.
Electrics, remoulds, a couple of scrapyards,
Roar of the living on the expressway,
Lift up your eyes to the hills and the empty sky.

House Clearance

When you were gone, widow in a childless house,
As smoke, as shadow of smoke and thin deposit of ash
Forgive us, we went from room to room under the roofspace
Lagged with woolly dust, under that head of cold
We gathered up your substance, all the leavings
And sorted this for us, this for charity, this for the tip
Breaking and entering on your privacy
We delved for what you might have hoarded among underwear
The orange chocolate biscuits, wallets of photographs
Wads of pension, documentations of a dead baby,
Hardening our hearts, impieties, impieties,
Even against the cards heart-shaped and red and quilted
Addressed to MAM from someone not your flesh
For Christmas, birthday and Mothering Sunday
That being opened down a score of years still chimed
Like mobiles in a wreck, but we
With coats and hats more than in C&A
More dresses than a run of Mothers' Union jumble sales
With orange cardigans and the summer blouses
That crush to nothing like a conjuror's bright scarves
We bloated the first black plastic bags
The grey dust in our hair, and rounded up
From where you had hidden them or they hid themselves
In hide-and-seek and nobody came seeking
The last of your rag and woolly tribe of dolls and animals
Already priced for charity, room by room until
From a wardrobe out flopped
A clown the size of a boy of five or six
Sewn in motley, stuffed and grinning, right as ninepence
And we blessed you for that, for giving us a thing
At once we could give away to the girl next door who asked,
Now you are gone, Was the house haunted? Yes, by love.

Shoes in the Charity Shop

It can't be helped, the way our minds turn
When we see worn shoes in a pile,
It is an evolution of our kind
We shan't grow out of. But this is charity
This widow pairing them along a rack and selecting
The worst for the tip, the better for pricing
And bringing out into the front shop
For the poor still walking
To step into. Noblest
Were those worn shoes of women queuing at the bus-stop
And along the pavement shuffling turn by turn
Nearer the counter and to being served
While above their hands
Gripped by the weight of bags and the worry over every penny
And far above their feet
Killing them in those trodden shoes
Gloriously they were squandering breath on stories
A wealth of natter and tattle
And answering back. Their shoes
Would never have passed from the pile to the front shop
So shaped to them, who never wanted charity,
No feet on earth after theirs would have fitted them.

New Year Behind the Asylum

There was the noise like when the men in droves
Are hurrying to the match only this noise was
Everybody hurrying to see the New Year in
In town under the clock but we, that once,

He said would I come our usual Saturday walk
And see it in out there in the open fields
Behind the asylum. Even on sunny days
How it troubled me more and more the nearer we got

And he went quiet and as if he was ashamed
For what he must always do, which was
Go and grip the bars of the iron gates and stand
Staring into the garden until they saw him.

They were like the animals, so glad and shy
Like overgrown children dressed in things
Handed down too big or small and they came in a crowd
And said hello with funny chunnering noises

And through the bars, looking so serious,
He put his empty hand out. But that night
We crept past quickly and only stopped
In the middle of the empty fields and there

While the clock in the square where the normal people stood
And all the clocks in England were striking twelve
We heard the rejoicings for the New Year
From works and churches and the big ships in the docks

So faint I wished we were hearing nothing at all
We were so far away in our black fields
I felt we might not ever get back again
Where the people were and it was warm, and then

Came up their sort of rejoicing out of the asylum,
Singing or sobbing I don't know what it was
Like nothing on earth, their sort of welcoming in
Another New Year and it was only then

When the bells and the cheerful hooters couldn't be heard
But only the inmates, only the poor mad people
Singing or sobbing their hearts out for the New Year
That he gripped me fast and kissed my hair

And held me in against him and clung on tight to me
Under a terrible number of bare stars
So far from town and the lights and house and home
And shut my ears against the big children crying

But listened himself, listened and listened
That one time. And I've thought since and now
He's dead I'm sure that what he meant was this:
That I should know how much love would be needed.

Ashes and Roses

She is size 10 again like the girl under her banns
But so disconsolate the falling of her hand
I worry the diamond will slip to the grey earth.

These are only the bare bones of roses
This is a garden of little twists of iron
The dressing of ash does not look nourishing.

Let me look away at the sunny hills and you
Look at nothing for a while against my heart.
You feel as breakable as things I have found on the hills

After the weather when their small frames are evident.
You need to put on again
The roses need to flower. Come home

To your empty house. He is more there than here

Visiting

In broad daylight going back again
Under the black poplars to the old way in,
Locus of the dream, naked somnambule
Puzzled at the iron gates, eyeing the pitbull,
Viewing the garden let go to ruin
And shrunk so small how was there room in there
For cricket, the bonfire, the giant snowman,
Flowers and produce and rustic between the two?

All I want to embrace in there I should pass right through
With my closing arms. Better abide
The time of the naked soul and then enter
Easily between the bars and while
The foul dog sleeps come into the multitude
Gathered in the shrunken garden who are as thin

As negatives. But I,
Thinnest letter, is an infinity.

Fine Soil

I've come looking for that unwarlike man
My father, in a khaki blouson
At work riddling soil a yard or so
From where the rowan was and isn't now.

From the terraces settling in a Sunshine Home
On virgin fields with no experience
Only *The Gardener's Enquire Within*
He spoke the words like equals, 'Fine Soil'
With shy authority as though come
Into something homely and holy by amazing chance.

Midnight dreamer, I see him in the sun
And that goodness, that tip of good spoil
Mounding like mole-tilth from a fine rain
So sweet to work and plunge the hands in,
Lovely to seed. It had body, unlike the thin
Ash whose every mote was body once.

Riddling the Strata

Terra nova, so what jigged on the grille
And wasn't let through was mostly alluvial
Rounded pebbles from the old conglomerates
From the old seas and breccia bits,
Undone old makings, and little erratics
Travelled from Cumberland on the boulder clay,
Grits and greywackes, flung on the waste pile.

Now if they'd let me in I'd kneel
Near the scarlet memory of the rowan berries
And riddle our stratum, let the fine soil away
And feel with fingertips for our deposits,
The fuselages of Lancasters,
Limbs and weapons of lead soldiers,
A dinky ambulance, alleys
Of clay, glass, steel, the thin lead sticks
Safely chambered in a propelling-pencil.

Shed

I fixed a good long splinter to a gun of wood
And round the shed's blind corner anticlockwise
Clockwise stuck my brother just beneath the eye.

Inside there hung a gasmask like a trophy head
And the Jack of All Trades, Master of None
(His verdict) stood at the workbench in the sun,
Between his lips bright glints of nails,
Mending the family's shoes. The glue and leather smells,
The leather being pared by a blade gone
Crescent from shaping round the soles and heels
Upended on the last. What ironmongery!
What scores of correct names for all the things you need!
And the Maker and Mender Extraordinary
Eye on the job under the gasmask's insect eyes
Safe in there while round the clock outside
Everything whirls in luck, the bad, the good.

The Dark Room

Black-out and a red light. Safe light
Not light enough to hurt what can't appear
In the light. In it the Trismegist
Amazed the novice and himself in equal measure.
He launched our fortune cards under the surface,
He slipped them under the fluid's skin
With fingertips. He rocked them. As the book said.
My head bowed, his over mine was bowed
And loved ones bodied up, at rest.

Be warned, present occupiers, when I am through the gate
Past the pitbull, the sacred rowan, the million
Million shimmering atoms of the shed
I'll seek the dark room in your living space,
Sackman arriving with an infinite
Capital and compound interest of negatives,
I'll dip and bath to life again my lives.

Streets

Twenty-seven from Waterloo Street
Two from Barlows Road
Five from Blackburn Buildings
Only one each from West Thompson Street
Cranbourne Street, Bright Street, Langshaw Street
And Gun Street.
These are not levels of fervour
Only how many homes
(Unfit for heroes)
Had men and boys to give.
Liverpool Street gave fifty-five
Among them six by the name of Allmark
And my mother's father
8571 Private J.W. Gleave
From number fifty-seven
On the corner with little Healey Street
That gave three:
Private S. Cooper
Private J. Flanagan
Sergeant C.H. Taylor.
Eliza Street likewise gave three, all Molineuxs
Ayr Street gave four, three of them Andersons.
They were all other ranks round here
Nothing bigger than a sergeant.
I counted thirty-seven streets
In a half-mile square
And of them none are left:
Not Ducie Place
Not Brighton Place
Not Willis Street
Not West Joseph Street that gave
Private G. Olive
Corporal F. Cassidy
Sergeant R. Seddon
Private T. McNulty
Nor Albion Street that gave
All three Bowkers.
The bit of Liverpool Street is left
That led to the abattoir

But not a home along it
Nor a church, a mission hall
A corner shop, a stables
Nor any pub but one
The Live and Let Live
Boarded up
And no list anywhere.

I counted two hundred and twenty-one men went from here

To Happy Valley
Nameless Wood
Krab Krawl
Stuff Trench
Hellblast Corner
And Dead Man's Dump.

Fields

On Cruthers, seaward abandoned
So long drenched with salt

Some paper whites
Delicate and plucky as butterflies in rusty wire
Rise every year in the wreckage of bracken and brambles

Three cists on the chine

But on the leeside
High winds can come over
And a man be there
In fields like roofless rooms
Head down quietly
And move up the soft furrows.

Jib Piece, the shape
The sweet curves of the rows
The old man's favourite
He said they could scatter him there but changed his mind
And lies above all the fields with the old lady

Dust and his bits of shrapnel.

Eastard.

Uncle Boss's, the black pine
In red-hot pokers and agapanthus.

John Batty's, a barrow
The cladding robbed for hedges
Strong unctuous earth
Which smelt cadaverous.

The Prison
Four high evergreen walls and so big
Picking or planting seems a long sentence (still
A vast allowance of sky, clouds travelling, sea on the doorstep
There are worse confinements).

The Dry Field.
Ferny Splat.
Enter Hills.

The Homeland
No pain, no death, no grief.

Little Eastard.
Cold Wind.

Adrianople
The wars of the Russians and the Turks.

Spion Kop
That went back long ago under brambles, bracken, gorse
The Christophers broke in
Under the moon
Ridding it of brambles, bracken, gorse
Dry hedging it with the spoil
But split from Cruthers
And dragged on a sledge
Two great orthostats
To be the gateway opening on a risen field
Of sols, avalanches, paper whites,
In 1900
For weddings, christenings and funerals
And named it after a battle
In the old tradition
Of native clay and foreign fields
At the opening of the age
Of bulk slaughter.

Eleven little islands
Can be seen from Spion Kop
They have the peace and the patience of animals
That all night under the stars
Are there and in the morning
Still when the mist lightens.

Sols, avalanches, paper whites
Mostly for funerals.

Girls in the East

These girls in their bits of bright skirt
Slung low on the down under their belly buttons
Show me a man in this place who could have fathered them
And among the women
Buttoned up stoutly in old clothes
Any likely mother.

The way they ride the trams of the Republic
The way they stride
They must be a generation of changelings
Such clear skin
You don't get that on a diet of five-hour speeches
Nor queuing round the walls in the acid drizzle of sadness.

Here comes an ancient father with his ageing son.
The father is scaly with medals
The son is trailing a flag
It was a demonstration in memory of the old days
Briefly their eyes shone like the medals
Briefly they stood up stiff as flagstaffs
Now they are going home to the old smells
Trapped on every landing
And matching wives and mothers.

Where did the bare-legged girls blow in from?

They must have seeded themselves
In cracks in the four-square mausoleum
In the clay of the feet of the Shepherds of the People
Or perhaps they were there all along
Under the square and the tanks went over them
And when the perishing of the concrete had begun
At the first tickling of illicit grass
Night after night like white foxgloves
Cool as moonlight
Hard as stars
These daughters of nowhere came up legion.

They have no memory
They have no piety
The dead in this place will have to bury themselves.

School Parties in the Museum

Daily the boroughs, hopeful as a flood tide,
Release some children and Miss and Sir
And several guardian angels conduct them without loss
Through the underground in crocodiles to here,
The Room of the Kings, with questionnaires.

What the Jew Bloom said was no use – force,
Hatred, history, all that – here
There's enough of it to wipe out everything that lives,
Enough Fathers of the People, enough Peace Lords
Among their deeds with a half-life of a million years.

Hurrying through from the Tea Room to the Reading Room
In drifts of children I could make no headway
But a space and a silence came into my mind
Among them crying like birds and flitting and settling
So that for once I saw a thing properly:

A thoughtful dot in socks and a white frock
Under the famous fist on its level length of arm,
Black granite fist, black as the people's blood is
When it has dried on the square in the usual sun,
Fist of some god or president, some wise

Dispenser of plagues of locusts and Agent Orange
And she was under it in pigtails with a clipboard
Pondering up at it in a space all on her own
As serious as the entire Reading Room
And black as a brand new question mark.

Daily for opening time and all day long
Till the last admission the ever hopeful boroughs send
Under the world's colours wave on wave
Of their bright fragments of the New Republic
Future present, with questions, against the Kings.

Jazz on the Charles Bridge
(for Si and Konni)

Go on, go on, I believe you, I believe
The big river, sick of dirt,
Sick of ferrying our murders to the dead sea,
Suddenly feels a kick like quickening
And this is the source come clean again at last

And now she will be well, encore, encore,
I believe it, the unnecessary
Saints and martyrs must pine away
Or raise their instruments like Mr Horn
Or strum like Thimble Fingers on the washboard

Or pluck like that one cuddling the bass, and croak
In Czech, oh, won't you please come home?
All is well now, all is forgiven, the Real
Republic is here, the best we'll ever get
And good, so good, such courtesy

The way they let one another through in turn,
The way they take him up again like the peloton
In a rush of applause of equals,
Go on, go on, no wonder the sun comes out
No wonder the wind kisses up little waves,

Oh, brothers and sisters, this is it
Builded here, Careless Love, and not
The blues but something more like a boy and a girl
Outstretched to one another on the high trapeze, for life
And death, their eyes in one another, laughing.

'Hölderlin'

('Hölderlin' was the code name used by an East German poet when she spied for the Stasi.)

Why? Because after you, what you had said,
What you had put about among humankind,
Even bigger lies were possible and on your highs
That deep came disappointment. After you

We lived like foreigners in our mother country
Among the trades and functions, among the shells
Not one inhabited by a living kind
Of human. There was always a word for us

Because of you, more than a word, the thing,
Your doing, that want, that powerless power
When faces lifted from the text and whispered 'Come
Into the open, friend, oh come, oh make

It true, the spirit quickening through all the veins
Of a republic's life, this very earth,
Ours here – if not now, when?' All that
In a mother country of old men, always

Men and old, the same old men and their
'Not now, not yet'. I sided with the liars
Against the disappointed, I wear your name
Emptily, like grief, like vain revolt.

Hallowe'en

1

Small cluster of our dead
Like a Pleiades, they change
Their quarter season by season
But never go below
For where we are they are.

Apples, lanterns, fire;
On the marsh behind the fire
Soft rollers of mist from the sea.
Come closer, friendly dead
Watch over the waiting house.

2

Little somebody
Eyes shut
You missed the eclipse
But never mind.

Along Mynydd Bach
On every knoll
And some at the trigpoint
And some at the cairns
Where the huddled small
Dead were housed
In good time
Watchers appeared
All innocent
Only watching.

It was like waking
Where you were dreaming
In the queer light
Russet and flickering
And utter silence
Where you were dreaming
Shoals of light
Over Llyn Eiddwen

And just in time
Came a high wind
A quiet commotion
And the sky opened:

Black sun
Black moon
Moon on the sun
And over the rim
Allowed by the moon
And moonshaped
A show of sun
The crowning edge
Of the terror of the rest:

Phenomenon

Little girl or boy
Us waiting know
And you'll soon see
Life here's
Like that
You lattice your eyes
With peeping fingers
And cloud is a mercy
When like that
That bright
Over the rim
The wishing crescent
Of love comes
And hooks the heart
Fast.

Skylight over the Bed

The two stars in the skylight must be Gemini.
Hard to be sure with constellations,
Time of the year, time of the night, and only that
Small window on their travelling, but here
Awake on another middle of a night,
Single the flesh again, single the mind
Again but biding in a patient watchfulness
And only puzzling for the fun of it
What else belongs around that little excerpt
Of silver dots on black, for now
Under the slant look of the loveless sky
As tranquil, almost, as a husband on a marble tomb
No more infringing on your state of sleep
Than little finger crooked in little finger
I'm pretty sure those two stars must be Gemini.

Skylight over the Bath

Starlight is good and a *voyeuse* moon
But daylight is better still and rain
And not a mizzle or a pitter patter
But Aquarius in person astride your ridge tiles
Emptying the urns of heaven down the slopes.

Being in water under water, can you remember
That far back, globule in a swimming mother,
Pod in a swamp somewhere? Or as a tot
Launched all alone in a crib for a boat
Hiding in a quiet pool behind the waterfall?

Full length and single in your snug billet
One thing you can see for yourself up there's
An acceleration of the molecules of glass
Which are slower than a glacier in your usual view.
Under the skim of water watch them come down fast.

That close the sisterhood of hard glass
And water, what hopes of lasting for you
Who are as watery as a lettuce, so they say?
No wonder the easeful Romans let out
Their blood in the bath to unboldly go that way.

Under the grisaille in the agapanthus blue
Voyager feet first in a chaste casket
Announcing yourself to the cold outside with gasps of steam
Leave through the wall like a babe of the *Enterprise*:
Longship, cuttlefish, speck in the salt foam.

Gorse

Keeps with its dead
Shows off by the bare facts of its dead
How hard it was
Living and how it triumphed and all winter
Among its own dead grizzle
Little moist lips of it go on muttering light.

It's the dead I've come for
Put in my naked hand among the spines and feel for
Anything springy I let be
To come on again and add its sparks to the rush of Easter and Whitsun
But the dead snaps off
There and then it can be broken up hearthsize
Lengths straight as flutes
Or curving open like welcomes
Or twirled like dance
For nothing burns like the limbs of gorse
So thoroughly dead
Twisted for breathing space
Drilled and cankered
Host to the hungers of other kinds of life
How they burn
All without fat and flesh and blood
Without dribble or mewling
So much flame in every stub of gorse
Millions of Easters and Whitsuns
The scent and yellow fume under blue skies
All that as flame
With the lights off
Rain and fog over the bit of terra firma
And on the hearthrug
Kneeling
Aquarius and Pisces
Amazed.

Fulmars

I go there most days for a look at mastery
Flat out, eyes over the edge
The warm stink of the ledges up my nose
And the sea far down, never quiet, always mulling over something.

They don't want me there, I make them nervous
But the mastery comes up on the nervousness
So close, light through the ruddering feet
Eyes like coals on a snowman
Breath in a bony housing

I see the wingbeats are a charge of energy
And the glide a sort of freewheeling
That carries to the crest of a long slope of air
And faster down again, but also I see
What else must be there

(Lovely the showing forth
By them
To us
What must be there)

A lift off the lifting sea
Palpable streamers in the empty air
Fender, bias, swing
From under the concave cliff

And the flick, the tilt, the tremor
All the while the eye on me
In a state of total attending
Of utter hearkening to the possibilities
These are continual corrections for best advantage
Of forces not available to me
Airs between the cliff and the sea

They come to the dot
Which is the place in time between thus far and next
And halt on that split second

Then away, sheerly away, for another charging.

All I can ever do is say what things are like
And what they are like is what they remind me of.

Looking down on flight
Or on the shadows of flight over the salt water
Up comes the ancient conviction that I could fly
All I had to do was remember how
Hours of practice off the garden wall
And though the arms were right
Stiff and tilting
And the eye was utterly fixed on the idea
How foolish under the Spitfire
The peddling legs
In the unhelpful air

The gliders my father made did better than that

I can see his hands, his eye on the job
Folding a sheet of paper for the head and wings
A little anxiety watching his own hands
Whether they still remembered how
And the smile when they did

(I thought it would come back to me when the time came
The knack
The man's origami)

Stiff wings, a tight beak
They launched eagerly
Seemed to be able to feel out the best airways
Close my eyes I can see them on a blue sky
Ride and circle
Fail gracefully in spirals

Still nothing like fulmars.

I could lie there for ever they would never get used to me
Always know me for a foreign body
And I could watch for ever and never get the hang of it

That economy
Everything to the point
Grace in the fitness.

By lamplight in the early mornings
I study my hands:
Somewhere between them and the head
And a sheet of ordinary paper
There is an old invention
Ghost wanting blood
Memory wanting precipitation
Thin air a shape
As keen on the heart as an icy lightning.

Close my eyes I can see the fulmars
Head on, coming in fast
Against gravity, silent
Fixed on my attention
As though by force of looking
The pull of love
Every atom hearkening
I could summon them up.

Orangery

1

The trees are coming in down the long aisle
One by one, always the farthest first, on a yellow fork-truck
Lifted as little as need be but like a gift
Or the lares and penates, like the ancestors

Seated, benign, or like the child
Wished for and watched for down the long *allée* to the very end
Arriving now, coming home
Into the warm, the winter house. There must be a music

As slow as a dead march, solemn but not in mourning
For this coming in of orange and oleander,
Lemon and pomegranate on a muffled day,
A pavane, in the slow tempo

Of accustomed transit. What will come. What has to be done.
What will happen if not. Without haste. In good time.
The long forethought. It is early days,
Last week there were swallows still, a long while yet

Till the fountains drop down dead, wood clads them, the lake
Shuts and in minus twenty
Plus windchill the rooted natives aspire
To the only condition for survival: iron.

Slower than a hearse meanwhile
Or a gun-carriage down the gravel mall
Slightly rustling
Into the big house come the delicate exiles.

2

In the terminus, in the grey-clear light
Under the nine windows they have scarcely begun receiving
And these arrivals, the first, from farthest,
When they make an entrance it is still a marvel

How big they are, brought in
And offered by a little yellow fork-lift
Lowered and left, as big as the statues
Brought down from high up under the tympanum. In here

The gardeners are busy barbers
On styles that over the season have reverted to the elemental
A work like grooming the beasts in the big houses
The human voice continuing in conversation

Along the flanks, over the still heads
Of other shapes of life, but softly, not to startle
And not to clash with the colours of the whole interior
The matt greens, the opal, the dull gold. High in the centre

That pair face to face across the apex of a double ladder
Stretching to round the crown of a *laurier-rose*
He has reached her the last bloom
For a lush pink buttonhole in her working blue

And although we can't see her face his is certain
That so much oblation of trimmings from the Greek trees
Has placated death for ever
And her open torch will see them through any winter.